The Urbana Free Library

To renew: call **217-367-4057**
or go to **urbanafreelibrary.org**
and select **My Account**

A LOOK AT CHEMISTRY

ATOMS

BY KENNON O'MARA

 Gareth Stevens
PUBLISHING

CRASHCOURSE

Please visit our website, www.garethstevens.com. For a free color catalog of all our high-quality books, call toll free 1-800-542-2595 or fax 1-877-542-2596.

Library of Congress Cataloging-in-Publication Data

Names: O'Mara, Kennon, author.
Title: Atoms / Kennon O'Mara.
Description: New York : Gareth Stevens Publishing, [2019] | Series: A look at chemistry | Includes index.
Identifiers: LCCN 2018014328| ISBN 9781538230107 (library bound) | ISBN 9781538231401 (pbk.) | ISBN 9781538233214 (6 pack)
Subjects: LCSH: Atoms--Juvenile literature. | Matter--Properties--Juvenile literature. | Chemistry--Juvenile literature.
Classification: LCC QC173.16 .O4225 2019 | DDC 541/.24--dc23
LC record available at https://lccn.loc.gov/2018014328

First Edition

Published in 2019 by
Gareth Stevens Publishing
111 East 14th Street, Suite 349
New York, NY 10003

Designer: Reann Nye
Editor: Therese Shea

Photo credits: Series art Marina Sun/Shutterstock.com; cover Sergey Nivens/Shutterstock.com; p. 5 locrifa/Shutterstock.com; p. 23 Zodar/Shutterstock.com; p. 25 Humdan/Shutterstock.com; p. 27 Kletr/Shutterstock.com; p. 29 chanchai howharn/Shutterstock.com.

Printed in the United States of America

CPSIA compliance information: Batch #CW19GS: For further information contact Gareth Stevens, New York, New York at 1-800-542-2595.

CONTENTS

Words in the glossary appear in **bold** type the first time they are used in the text.

BUILDING BLOCKS

If you've ever played with building blocks, you know a bit about how atoms work already. They're the building blocks of nature. In fact, everything in nature is made up of the tiny **particles** called atoms!

MAKE THE GRADE

The word "atom" comes from the Greek word *atomos*, which means "that which can't be split."

INSIDE THE ATOM

Atoms are the smallest particles of matter, but they're made up of tinier bits called electrons, protons, and neutrons. Because they're smaller than atoms, electrons, protons, and neutrons are called subatomic particles. They're found in certain places within atoms.

ATOM

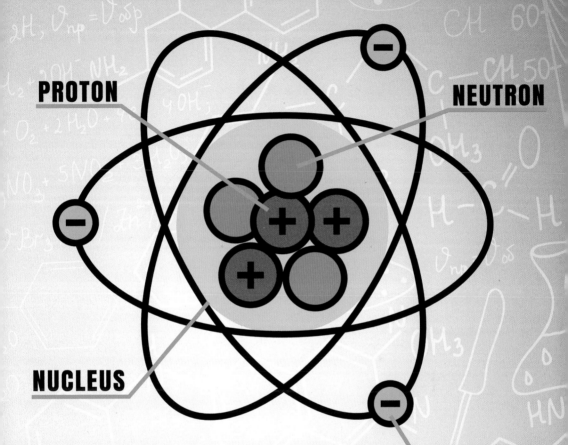

PROTON

NEUTRON

NUCLEUS

ELECTRON

MAKE THE GRADE

Scientists have discovered that subatomic particles are made up of even smaller bits! Protons and neutrons are made up of particles called quarks.

Every atom has a center called a nucleus. It's made up of protons and neutrons. Electrons **orbit** the nucleus, a bit like Earth orbits the sun! They surround the nucleus in pathways called shells or energy levels.

IRON ATOM

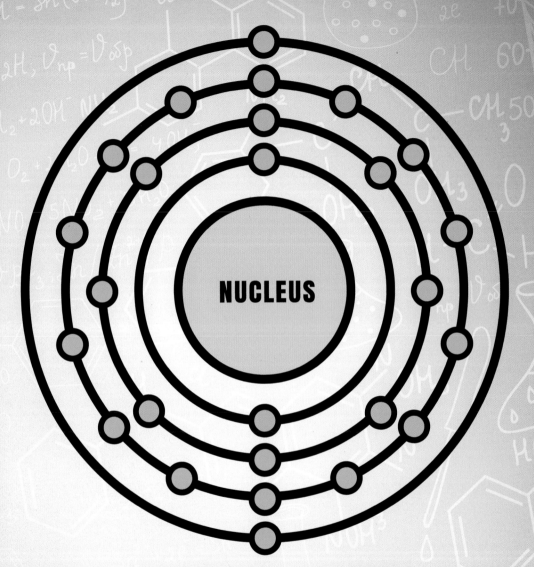

NUCLEUS

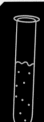

MAKE THE GRADE

Scientists use the letters K, L, M, N, O, P, and Q to label each shell. The "K" shell is closest to the nucleus, and "Q" is the farthest.

9

CHARGED UP

Both protons and electrons have the same amount of electric charge. However, protons have a positive charge and electrons have a negative charge. Particles with opposite charges **attract**. Particles with like charges **repel**. Neutrons carry no charge.

OPPOSITE CHARGES ATTRACT

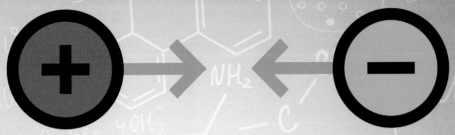

LIKE CHARGES REPEL

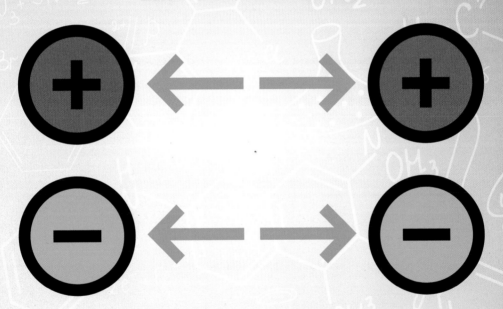

 MAKE THE GRADE

When an atom has an equal number of protons and electrons, it has no overall electric charge. However, that can change.

Electrons travel around the nucleus in their shells. However, they can break free. Sometimes they join other atoms. This changes the overall charge of the atom the electron left as well as the atom it joins.

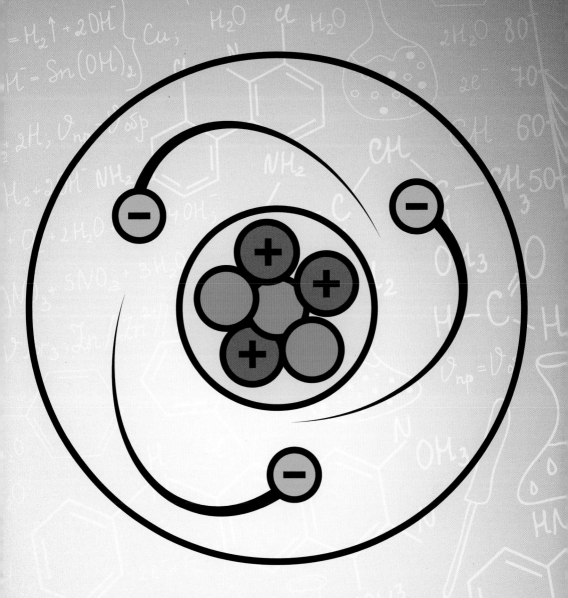

MAKE THE GRADE

Not all shells hold the same
number of electrons. It depends
on the kind of atom.

Atoms lose or gain electrons
in **chemical reactions**
or when they crash into
other atoms. An atom that
loses an electron becomes
positively charged. An
atom that gains an electron
becomes negatively
charged. Charged atoms
are called ions.

NEGATIVE ION

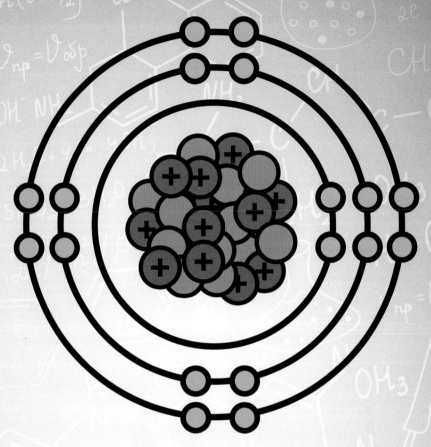

- **+** 17 PROTONS
- ◯ 18 NEUTRONS
- ⊖ 18 ELECTRONS

MAKE THE GRADE

The attracting force between protons and electrons is what keeps electrons in orbit around the nucleus—but they can still break free.

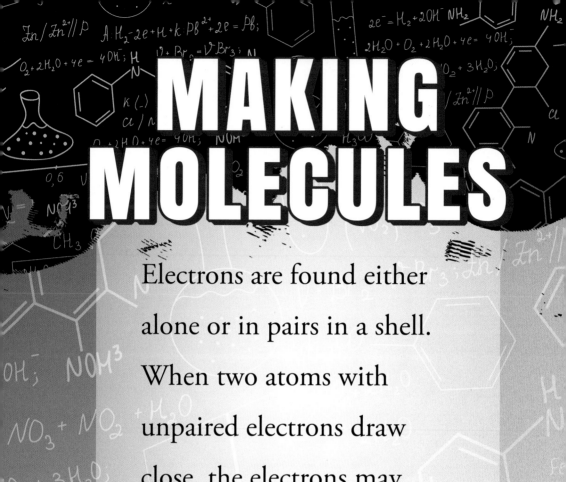

MAKING MOLECULES

Electrons are found either alone or in pairs in a shell. When two atoms with unpaired electrons draw close, the electrons may form a pair. The atoms then share the paired electrons. The atoms form what's called a molecule.

METHANE MOLECULE

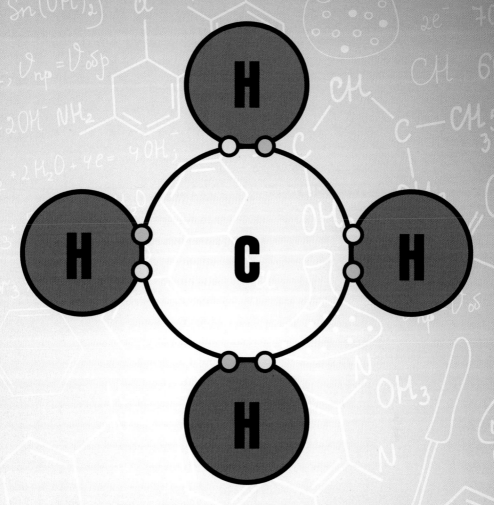

- 🔴 **ELECTRON FROM CARBON ATOM**
- ⚪ **ELECTRON FROM HYDROGEN ATOM**

 **MAKE THE GRADE**

Atoms with unfilled outer shells are **unstable**. They'll seek a bond with other atoms to become stable.

More than 90 types of atoms are found in nature. Each is an element. A pure element is only one type of atom. For example, molecules of hydrogen contain only hydrogen atoms. Molecules with atoms of two or more elements are called compounds.

THE COMPOUND H$_2$O

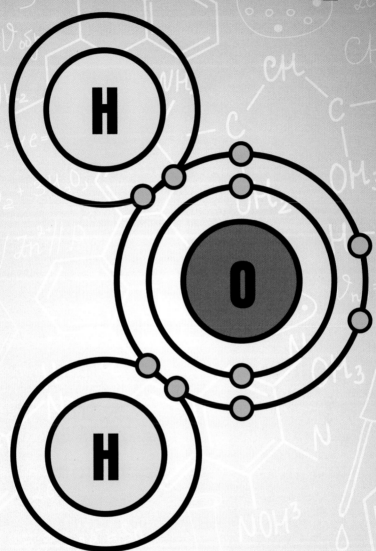

MAKE THE GRADE

Water, sometimes called H$_2$O, is a compound of hydrogen and oxygen atoms. Molecules can be made up of hundreds of thousands of atoms!

The link between atoms in a molecule is called a chemical bond. A bond between two nonmetal atoms is a covalent bond. A bond between metals and nonmetals is an ionic bond. Bonds that connect metal atoms are called metallic bonds.

COVALENT BONDS

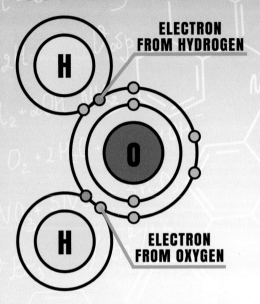

ELECTRON FROM HYDROGEN

H

O

H

ELECTRON FROM OXYGEN

IONIC BONDS

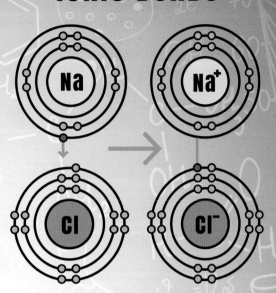

Na

Na⁺

Cl

Cl⁻

METALLIC BONDS

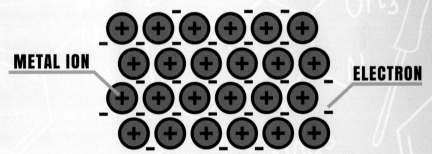

METAL ION

ELECTRON

 MAKE THE GRADE

All compounds are molecules,
but not all molecules
are compounds!

TO THE TABLE

The number of protons in an atom is called its atomic number. Every element has a **unique** atomic number. Elements are in order in the **periodic table** according to this number. As of April 2018, there are 118 chemical elements in the periodic table.

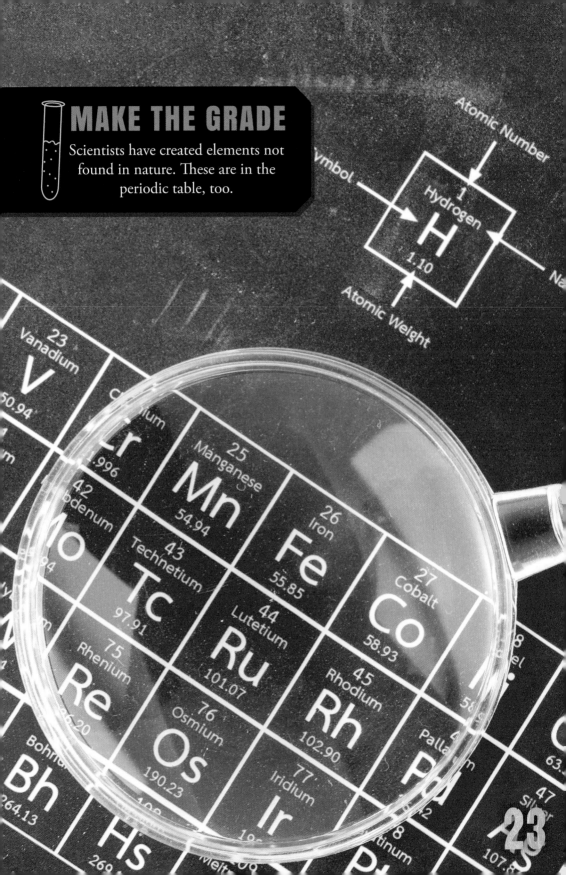

MAKE THE GRADE

Scientists have created elements not found in nature. These are in the periodic table, too.

Atomic Number

Symbol

1
Hydrogen
H
1.10

Na

Atomic Weight

23
Vanadium
V
50.94

25
Manganese
Mn
54.94

26
Iron
Fe
55.85

27
Cobalt
Co
58.93

.996

Cr

42
odenum
Mo
94

43
Technetium
Tc
97.91

44
Lutetium
Ru
101.07

45
Rhodium
Rh
102.90

Palla

75
Rhenium
Re
.20

76
Osmium
Os
190.23

77
Iridium
Ir

Bohr
Bh
264.13

Hs
269

Meit

47
Silver
107.8

Atomic mass is the number of protons and neutrons in an atom. Atomic weight is the **average** mass of an element's atoms in nature. Atomic weight is on many periodic tables. The mass and weight are measured in atomic mass units.

Periodic Table of the Elements

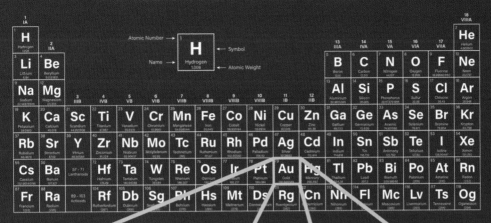

79

Au

Gold

196.966569

ATOMIC NUMBER

ATOMIC SYMBOL

ELEMENT

ATOMIC WEIGHT

 MAKE THE GRADE

Not all atoms of an element have the same mass. Isotopes are the same type of atom with a different number of neutrons.

ATOMIC ENERGY

Atoms are the basic building blocks of nature, but they can be split. When the nucleus of an atom splits into two or more parts, nuclear fission takes place. It produces a great amount of energy, or power. Nuclear fission in power plants is used to create electricity.

NUCLEAR POWER PLANT

 MAKE THE GRADE

Nuclear fission is also used to make
nuclear **weapons**.

The nuclei of two atoms can also be fused, or joined. This process is called nuclear fusion. It, too, creates a lot of energy. Nuclear fusion happens naturally in stars. That's how our sun gives off light and heat. Atoms are amazing!

MAKE THE GRADE

Inside the sun, nuclear fusion happens as hydrogen atoms fuse. They're turned into helium atoms.

THE STRUCTURE OF A NITROGEN ATOM

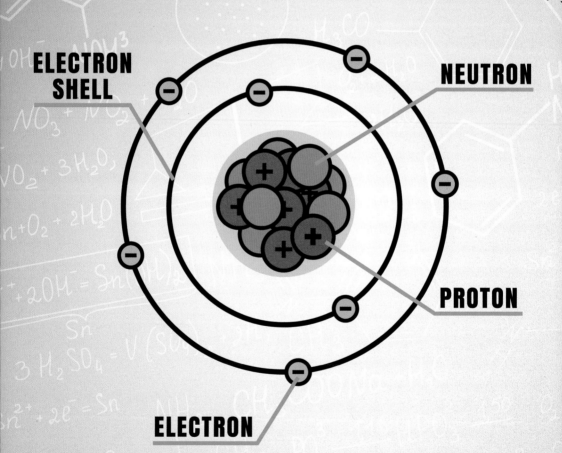

ELECTRON SHELL

NEUTRON

PROTON

ELECTRON

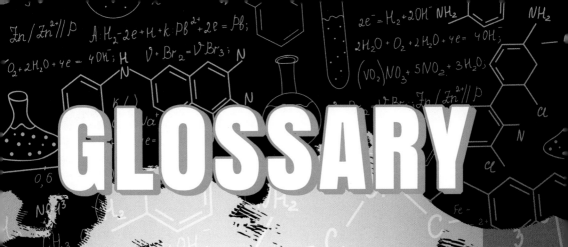

GLOSSARY

attract: to draw nearer

average: a number that is found by adding amounts together and then dividing the total by the number of amounts

chemical reaction: a change that occurs when two or more kinds of matter combine to form a new kind

orbit: to travel in a circle or oval around something, or the path used to make that trip

particle: a very small piece of something

periodic table: a list that shows the chemical elements arranged according to their properties

repel: to keep away

unique: one of a kind

unstable: having a state that changes easily

weapon: something used for fighting or attacking

FOR MORE INFORMATION

BOOKS

Dickmann, Nancy. *Energy from Nuclear Fission: Splitting the Atom*. New York, NY: Crabtree Publishing Company, 2016.

Paris, Morgaine. *Composition of Matter*. Huntington Beach, CA: Teacher Created Materials, 2016.

WEBSITES

Atoms

www.brainpop.com/science/matterandchemistry/atoms/
Watch a movie about atoms.

What Is an Atom?

www.livescience.com/37206-atom-definition.html
Learn more about atoms and the scientists who helped us discover more about them.

Publisher's note to educators and parents: Our editors have carefully reviewed these websites to ensure that they are suitable for students. Many websites change frequently, however, and we cannot guarantee that a site's future contents will continue to meet our high standards of quality and educational value. Be advised that students should be closely supervised whenever they access the internet.

INDEX